C0-DUY-215

A GIFT FOR:

FROM:

Published by Hallmark Gift Books,
a division of Hallmark Cards, Inc.,
Kansas City, MO 64141
Visit us on the Web at Hallmark.com.

All scriptures, unless otherwise noted, are taken from the Holy Bible, New International Version®, NIV®. Copyright © 1973, 1978, 1984, 2011 by Biblica, Inc.® Used by permission of Zondervan. All rights reserved worldwide. www.zondervan.com. The "NIV" and "New International Version" are trademarks registered in the United States Patent and Trademark Office by Biblica, Inc.®

Scripture from the New King James Version. Copyright © 1982 by Thomas Nelson, Inc. Used by permission. All rights reserved.

Editorial Director: Delia Berrigan
Editor: Kim Schworm Acosta
Art Director: Chris Opheim
Designer: Ren-Whei Harn
Production Designer: Dan Horton
Writer: Suzanne Berry

ISBN: 978-1-63059-691-0
1BOK1504

Made in China
1119

FINDING
GOD IN THE
Garden

Hallmark

"This is my Father's world,
And to my listening ears
All nature sings, and round me rings
The music of the spheres."

"This is My Father's World," Maltbie Davenport Babcock

Again he said, "What shall we say the kingdom of God is like, or what parable shall we use to describe it? It is like a mustard seed, which is the smallest of all seeds on earth. Yet when planted, it grows and becomes the largest of all garden plants, with such big branches that the birds can perch in its shade."

Mark 4:30-32

Hope can grow wherever it is planted.

The Lord God took the man and put him in the Garden of Eden to work it and *take care* of it.

Genesis 2:15

But if we *hope* for
what we do not yet have,

we wait for it *patiently.*

Romans 8:25

God sends a *rainy season* before the season of *growing begins.*

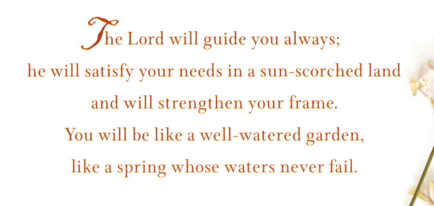

*T*he Lord will guide you always;
he will satisfy your needs in a sun-scorched land
and will strengthen your frame.
You will be like a well-watered garden,
like a spring whose waters never fail.

Isaiah 58:11

Blessings appear

IN GOD'S TIMING,
NOT OURS.

SO WE WAIT,

learning patience, having faith,

and trusting He is working

in our lives and in the world . . .

sometimes in ways

we can't yet see.

Every flower is a soul

blossoming

in nature.

— Gérard de Nerval

BEHOLD!

*F*or it is in nurturing that we are nurtured;

it is in conserving that we are conserved;

it is in loving Your earth,

and all that is in it,

that we truly show our love for You.

Fear
and *worry*

can pop up like weeds . . .

creeping in from all sides,

competing for our energy,

attention, and time.

Left alone, they'll take over.

But if we see them for what they are,

and carefully weed them out,

the good things God's planted

in each of us can breathe,

deepen, and thrive.

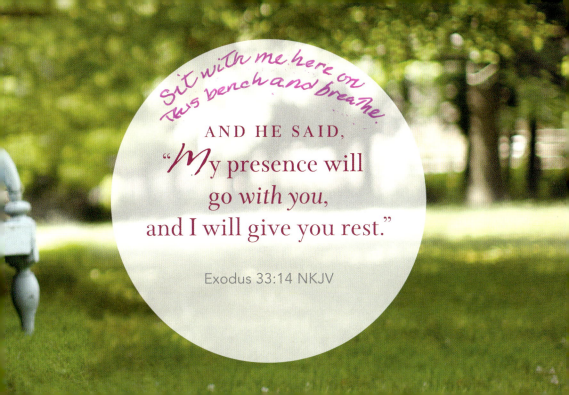

Sit with me here on this bench and breathe.

AND HE SAID,

"My presence will go with you, and I will give you rest."

Exodus 33:14 NKJV

Like flowers,

none of us became

who we are on our own.

Along the way,

God gave each of us

the nourishment we needed . . .

RAIN to deepen our roots,

SUN to open us in new directions,

and SWEET FRIENDS to visit our lives

and leave us forever changed.

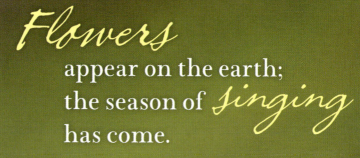

Flowers appear on the earth;
the season of *singing*
has come.

Song of Songs 2:12

One of my favorite songs –
Can you sing with me?

$\mathcal{I}$ come to the garden alone,

While the dew is still on the roses;

And the voice I hear, falling on my ear,

The Son of God discloses.

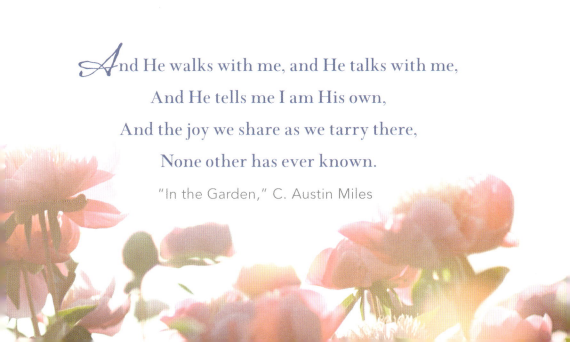

And He walks with me, and He talks with me,

And He tells me I am His own,

And the joy we share as we tarry there,

None other has ever known.

"In the Garden," C. Austin Miles

REJOICE!

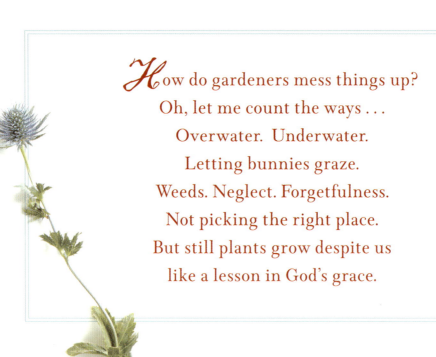

How do gardeners mess things up?
Oh, let me count the ways . . .
Overwater. Underwater.
Letting bunnies graze.
Weeds. Neglect. Forgetfulness.
Not picking the right place.
But still plants grow despite us
like a lesson in God's grace.

Heaven is
under our feet

as well as over our heads.

Henry David Thoreau

Give freely
of what you have.
With God, there will
always be more.

*A*ll things bright and beautiful,
All creatures great and small,
All things wise and wonderful,
The Lord God made them all.

Each little flow'r that opens,
Each little bird that sings,
He made their glowing colors,
He made their tiny wings.

"All Things Bright and Beautiful," Cecil Frances Alexander

𝒴ou will show me the path of life;

In Your presence *is* fullness of joy;

At Your right hand *are* pleasures forevermore.

Psalm 16:11 NKJV

Gratitude is a soil
on which *joy* thrives.

Berthold Auerbach

BE PRESENT
in this moment,
in this world.
All around are
beautiful blessings,
hidden in plain sight.

See how the flowers of the field grow.

They do not labor or spin.

Matthew 6:28

Nature
is the living,
visible garment
of God.

Johann Wolfgang von Goethe

*D*raw near to God,

and He will draw near to you.

James 4:8 NKJV

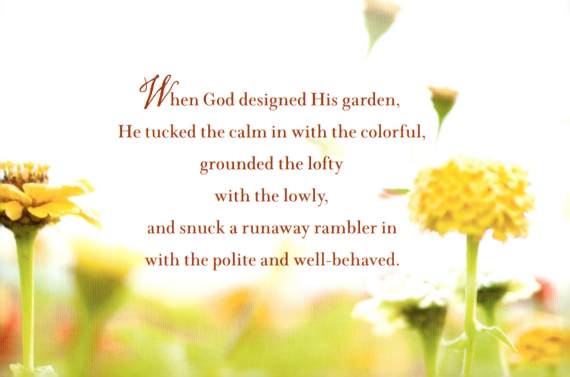

When God designed His garden,
He tucked the calm in with the colorful,
grounded the lofty
with the lowly,
and snuck a runaway rambler in
with the polite and well-behaved.

*B*ut that's just God for you . . .

surrounding us not

with more of the same,

but with what we need

to bring out each other's best,

find balance, and grow.

To everything *there* is a season,
A time for every purpose under heaven:
A time to be born,
And a time to die;
A time to plant,
And a time to pluck *what* is planted.

Ecclesiastes 3:1-2 NKJV

Create in me a pure heart, O God,

and renew a
steadfast *spirit*
within me.

Psalm 51:10

How Great Thou Art

I have come that
they may have life,
and have it to the full.

John 10:10

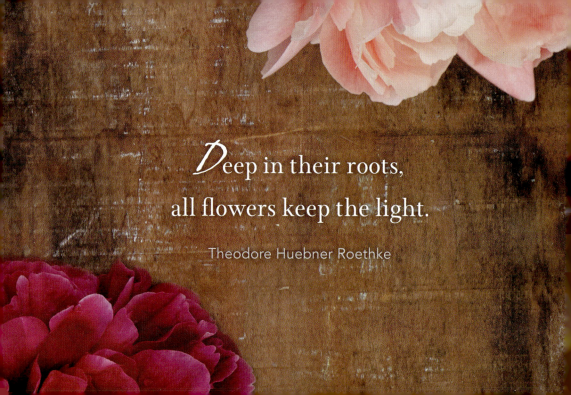

*D*eep in their roots,

all flowers keep the light.

Theodore Huebner Roethke

*W*inter visits each of us,

but that is not the end.

Spring will keep its promises.

It always comes, my friend.

Shall *flourish* in the courts of our God.

Psalm 92:13 NKJV

A Gardener's Prayer

A garden filled with summer
Where the blooming never ends,
A place to dream and putter
And to share with some old friends,
A place of grace and glory
The Lord has set apart,
A garden filled with summer–
That's heaven in my heart.

Ed Cunningham

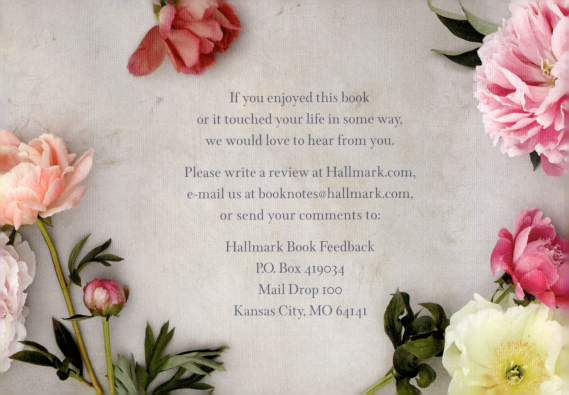

If you enjoyed this book
or it touched your life in some way,
we would love to hear from you.

Please write a review at Hallmark.com,
e-mail us at booknotes@hallmark.com,
or send your comments to:

Hallmark Book Feedback
P.O. Box 419034
Mail Drop 100
Kansas City, MO 64141